MIGRANTS AND REFUGEES

UNDERSTANDING GLOBAL ISSUES

Published by Smart Apple Media
1980 Lookout Drive
North Mankato, Minnesota 56003
USA

This book is based on *Migrants and Refugees: Millions of People on the Move*
Copyright ©1996 Understanding Global Issues Ltd., Cheltenham, England.

UGI Series Copyright ©2004 WEIGL PUBLISHERS INC.

Library of Congress Cataloging-in-Publication Data
Smith, Trevor.
Migrants and refugees / Trevor Smith.
    v. cm. -- (Understanding global issues)
Includes bibliographical references and index.
Contents: Introduction -- Migration and Civilization -- Escaping from war -- Economic
pressures -- Politics, ethnicity, religion -- Natural and man-made disaster -- Trafficking in
migrants -- Prevention and cure.
  ISBN 1-58340-360-4 (lib. bdg. : alk. paper)
 1. Refugees--Juvenile literature. 2. Immigrants--Juvenile literature. 3. Emigration and
immigration--Juvenile literature. [1. Refugees. 2. Immigrants. 3. Emigration and
immigration.] I. Title. II. Series.
  HV640.S65 2004
  325--dc21

                                    2003000113

                          Printed in Malaysia
                          2 4 6 8 9 7 5 3 1

EDITOR Donald Wells **COPY EDITOR** Heather Kissock
TEXT ADAPTATION Trevor Smith **DESIGNER** Terry Paulhus
PHOTO RESEARCHERS Tracey Carruthers, Pamela Wilton, and Peggy Chan
LAYOUT Terry Paulhus **SERIES EDITOR** Jennifer Nault
CREATIVE COMPANY EDITOR Jill Weingartz

Contents

Introduction

Every year, millions of people move away from their homes and communities. Some people leave because they are looking for a better life, but millions of people are forced to flee their homes because of war, persecution, or disaster.

People who move by choice are called migrants. Those who are driven out of their homes by war, persecution, or disaster are called refugees. In 2000, the International Organization for Migrants (IOM) reported that the number of people moving worldwide had reached 150 million, or 3 percent of the world's population. About 20 million of these people were refugees.

Human history is a story of **migration**, and there are four main reasons why people migrate: war; economic pressure; political, ethnic, and religious persecution; and natural disasters.

During the last 100 years, millions of people have migrated by choice or to escape war, persecution, or disaster. Millions of people were displaced by the breakup of the Ottoman Empire in the early part of the 20th

In Africa alone, more than 13 million people were displaced in 2000 as a result of violence, persecution, and famine.

century. The upheavals of World Wars I and II led to massive movements of people around the world. The partition of India from 1946 to 1947 caused the resettlement of 10 to 15 million people as Hindus moved into India and Muslims moved into Pakistan. The breakup of the Soviet Union created a new wave of **immigration** in the 1990s.

Before the 16th century, people could move from one country to another without passports. As **nations** began to take shape, governments started to control the movement of people, and passports or other documents were needed to cross international borders.

People still need passports to move from country to country, but globalization is breaking down the idea of nation. Ideas and products can cross borders without passports, and cultures are mixing more than ever.

Although many nations are now trying to slow the rate of migration, the increasing flow of goods, money, and services across borders is having a profound effect on immigration. In a world that is fast becoming a global village, the movement of people from country to country cannot be stopped.

It is a basic human right for people to live wherever they please. While most people prefer to stay in their home countries, if it is not possible for them to live safely or to have a decent life, migration may be their only choice. The challenge is to honor people's right to live where they choose without the social chaos created by large numbers of people moving from one country to another.

FORCED TO LEAVE

The number of people who have been forced to leave their homes and communities due to war, persecution, and natural disaster has increased dramatically over the last 50 years.

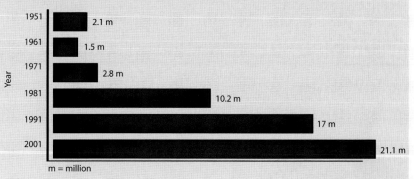

Year	
1951	2.1 m
1961	1.5 m
1971	2.8 m
1981	10.2 m
1991	17 m
2001	21.1 m

m = million

Migration and Civilization

Most countries are made up of immigrants or people whose ancestors were immigrants. The United States, for example, is comprised entirely of immigrants and descendants of immigrants.

Even Native Americans, the original residents of the U.S., are thought to be from Asia. According to this widely held theory, the ancestors of modern-day Native Americans came to North America 15,000 to 35,000 years ago. Although the mass immigration of Europeans to the U.S. brought European culture to North America, it created shock waves that almost destroyed the Native Americans and their culture.

In 1942, Robert Lindneux painted *The Trail of Tears*. This painting commemorates the suffering endured by the Cherokee people when they were forced to move from their homes in the 1800s.

By the time the Europeans arrived in the 15th century, there were millions of native people living throughout North, Central, and South America. More and more Europeans arrived—50 million Europeans migrated in the 1900s alone, most of them coming to the United States.

As a result, Native Americans were pushed onto reservations or forced to give up their way of life and become part of the new society. Others were forced to move far from their homelands.

The infamous Trail of Tears is an example of Native Americans being forced to move far from home. Between 1790 and 1830, the population of the state of Georgia increased six-fold. This increase in population created a problem—land for homesteading was becoming scarce. The Cherokee who lived in Georgia had started to become part of the new culture, but the Indian Removal Act of 1830 allowed new settlers to force them off their lands. Most of the Cherokee were put into makeshift forts and then forced to march 1,000 miles (1,609 km) west. On the first march, more than 4,000 people died, many of them women and children. The process was repeated with other Native Americans, and by 1840, more than 70,000 native people were forced to move from their homeland.

The modern state of Israel serves as another example of how immigration can cause problems for the original residents of an area. The state of Israel was founded in 1948, and since then, millions of Jewish people have moved into the area because they believe it is their homeland. The Palestinian Arabs, who have lived in this part of the world for centuries, also see it as their homeland. As

---

Immigration can cause trouble for the original residents of an area.

---

more Jewish people have arrived, more Palestinians have moved out, many of them becoming refugees. This migration and displacement has led to a conflict that has been going on for more than 50 years. Although Jewish people and Arabs lived side by side in the past, the founding of the state of Israel has created strange patterns of migration, with many people entering and many people leaving.

ETHNIC COMMUNITIES

Many cities have entire communities where the residents are mainly from one culture. Chinatown in San Francisco and Little Italy in New York are famous examples of ethnic communities. Immigrants often wish to keep close ties with people from their original communities, and they try to recreate their homeland in the new country. Some people do not support these types of communities. They feel that new immigrants should blend into their new countries instead of separating themselves in ethnic communities. Other people say that these ethnic communities are important because they preserve the culture and add variety to a city.

New York City and San Francisco have the largest Chinatowns in North America. These ethnic communities are major tourist attractions that generate jobs and enable people to learn about Chinese culture.

These types of forced movements of people and the suffering they cause have been repeated many times in human history. For example, 12 million Africans were forced to move during the age of slavery, and as many as 30 million **indentured** workers from the European colonies migrated between 1850 and 1939.

Urbanization and the globalization of business, finance, telecommunications, travel, and entertainment are affecting labor and migration, although the reasons people move have not changed. People are still forced to move because of war, persecution, and disaster, but most people are migrating in search of a better life for themselves and their families. As the mixing of people from different cultures continues to grow, more countries are becoming **multi-ethnic** and **multicultural**. Perhaps this mixing of cultures will help reduce ethnic prejudice and the risk of war.

KEY CONCEPTS

Globalization During the latter half of the 20th century, new information and communication technologies, such as the Internet, combined with new trends in international commerce to help create an interconnected world.

Migrants Migrants are people who move from one country to another. Emigration occurs when people move away from their home country, and immigration occurs when they move into their new countries. Migrants move by choice. They are not driven away from their homes by danger or persecution. A person may decide to migrate for any number of reasons, but most people migrate in search of better jobs and better lives for themselves and their families.

Refugees Refugees are people who are forced to leave their homes. The United Nations (UN) defines a refugee as a "person outside of his or her country of nationality who is unable or unwilling to return because of persecution or a well-founded fear of persecution on account of race, religion, nationality, membership in a particular social group, or political opinion." The number of refugees worldwide has increased dramatically over the past 50 years, growing from 2.2 million in 1955 to 20 million in 2002.

Immigration Information Officer

Duties: Aids immigrants with information and services

Education: Government-designed residential programs that can last from 5 to 20 weeks. Degrees in other disciplines, such as anthropology or social work, are recommended

Interests: Helping people, working in government

Navigate to the Immigration and Naturalization Service Web site **www.ins.usdoj.gov** for more information about a career as an immigration official. Also, click on **www.immigration.about.com** for more information about immigration issues.

Careers in Focus

Each year, hundreds of thousands of people try to enter the United States looking for a better life. These people need help applying for citizenship, applying for benefits under the Immigration and Nationality Act, and looking for information about their new home. This is the duty of an immigration information officer, a career that requires 5 to 20 weeks of residential training.

There are many different jobs within the United States Immigration and Naturalization Service. These jobs include information officer, criminal investigator (special agent), deportation officer, adjudications officer, immigration inspector, immigration agent (enforcement), asylum officer, border patrol agent (BPA), and detention enforcement officer (DEO). Each job requires people with different skills, but they all have the same goal: regulating and managing the flow of immigrants into the United States.

Escaping from War

In the developed world, war is difficult to understand. Money and politics have replaced civil war as a way to gain power in the developed world. In the developing world, civil war is still common.

Since World War II, most wars have been **civil wars** rather than wars between countries, but this has not made it any easier for the people affected by these conflicts. In fact, the opposite is true. A war against another country may bring people together and build community spirit, which can bind a nation together. When neighbors fight each other, community spirit and social trust disappear.

Armed conflicts such as civil wars have caused a large loss of life. UNICEF (United Nations Children's Fund) claims that about two million children were killed and six million children were seriously injured or permanently disabled in wars fought during the 1990s. Another 12 million children have

The breakup of the Yugoslavian federation resulted in civil wars that created an estimated 2.7 million refugees and displaced people in the early part of the 1990s. Many of these people had nowhere to go because their homes had been bombed or burned.

become homeless. In order to protect children in areas that are experiencing armed conflicts, UNICEF has called for a ban on anti-personnel land mines and an end to the **conscription** and recruitment of children under the age of 18 into military forces.

The presence of children armed with lightweight weapons such as AK-47s—sold in Africa for as little as $6.00 each—has complicated the refugee problem. An orphaned child armed with a gun has a better chance of survival, and although aid agencies try to provide children affected by war with food, shelter, and education, some child victims of war have learned to kill for food.

The conflict in the Great Lakes region of central Africa

Money and politics have replaced civil war as a way to gain power in the developed world.

---

has taken death and destruction to new levels. Between 500,000 and 800,000 people were killed in the 1994 **genocide** in Rwanda.

Around two million people fled the conflict, and about 80,000 people died in the refugee camps set up in Zaire, Tanzania, and Rwanda—50,000 in one month. That disaster brought a massive and immediate **humanitarian** response from the international community. Between April and December 1994, about $1.4 billion was spent to bring aid to the refugees. At least 7 UN agencies, approximately 250 **nongovernmental organizations** (NGOs), the Red Cross and Red Crescent, and at least 8 military groups were involved in the relief effort.

THE COLLAPSE OF COMMUNISM

The sudden collapse of communism in the Soviet Union and other Eastern European countries at the beginning of the 1990s displaced millions of people. Nearly 200,000 people were displaced in the Chechnya region, and the war in the former Yugoslavia created three million refugees. Also, many former Soviet citizens in Central Asia have moved because of the creation of new countries.

PALESTINIAN REFUGEES

The conflict between Israel and Palestine has been going on for more than 50 years. During this conflict, many Palestinians have been driven from their homes into Israeli-controlled camps. These camps, meant to be temporary, have endured along with the conflict. The United Nations Relief and Works Agency for Palestine Refugees (UNRWA) supports these refugee camps with a budget of $173 million a year. This money is used to provide food, medical supplies, shelter, and jobs to 3.8 million Palestinian refugees.

AFGHANISTAN

The Soviet Union invaded Afghanistan in 1979. As a result, 6.2 million Afghan refugees fled to Pakistan, Iran, and other nearby countries. With help from the U.S. military, Soviet troops were forced to withdraw in 1989. By this time, half of all Afghans had been displaced by the violence. Civil war gripped the country until 1996, when Taliban forces took over the government. In October 2001, the U.S. and Britain attacked the Taliban, which had refused to hand over Osama bin Laden, a wanted international terrorist. This conflict was responsible for 3.5 million refugees and one million displaced people.

Whether the renewal of conflict in Africa and new refugee emergencies in the region will evoke a similar humanitarian response remains to be seen. Other countries may believe that Africa has to sort out its own problems. Unfortunately, this belief may result in an even greater loss of life than in 1994, and the international political involvement that may be needed to solve refugee problems on this scale seems as far away as ever.

▬▬ **During times of civil unrest and in the aftermath of natural disasters, the Red Cross provides humanitarian aid to refugees and displaced people.**

MODERN ARMED CONFLICTS

Algeria	Victory by the Islamic Salvation Front in the 1991 elections led to a military takeover. There has been civil war ever since.
Angola	A war of independence began in the 1960s, turning into civil war after the Portuguese left in 1975. A UN-brokered peace deal and elections brought an end to the conflict in 2002.
Armenia/ Azerbaijan	War broke out in 1992 over a border dispute and ended in 1994.
Cambodia	Civil war between 1975 and 1993 has been followed by an uneasy peace.
Chechnya	After the breakup of the Soviet Union, Chechens renewed their struggle for independence but have faced massive military action from Russia.
Colombia	Local wars between political factions began in the 1950s. In recent years, there has been civil war between government forces and the private armies of the drug barons.
East Timor	East Timor was **annexed** by Indonesia after Portugal left in 1975. Around 200,000 people were massacred at that time. A war of resistance ended with the independence of East Timor in 2002.
Eritrea/ Ethiopia	Civil unrest led to the ousting of Emperor Haile Selassie in 1974, but civil war continued until 1991. Eritrea was granted independence in 1993.
Guatemala	A low-level civil war has been going on since the mid-1950s between government forces and rebel peasant groups.
India/ Pakistan	Since 1949, UN observers have been monitoring the Kashmir border between India and Pakistan. These two countries came close to full-scale war in 2002.
Iraq	For many years, Iraq has been fighting an internal war against Kurds and Marsh Arabs.

KEY CONCEPTS

International Red Cross and Red Crescent Movement
Established in 1863 in Geneva, Switzerland, the Red Cross and Red Crescent (IRCRC) is a global humanitarian organization. It is nonpolitical, nondenominational, and nondiscriminatory to those in need. It acts as a neutral referee between warring parties, and it watches to make sure that prisoners of war are treated according to the Geneva Convention. IRCRC is the largest agency of its kind, and it has a vast amount of experience dealing with emergencies and disasters.

UNRWA (The United Nations Relief and Works Agency)
UNRWA was established in 1949 as a temporary, nonpolitical organization to provide services to more than 750,000 Palestinians who had lost their homes and jobs as a result of the Arab-Israeli war of 1948. Still operating after 50 years, UNRWA sets up and maintains dozens of schools and health centers in refugee camps in the Middle East.

Iraq/ United States	In 1991, the United States and many of its allies pushed Iraqi forces out of the small country of Kuwait.
Israel/ Palestinians	Conflict between Israel and Palestine has been going on since 1948, sometimes spilling over into Jordan, Egypt, Lebanon, and Syria.
Liberia	Civil war began in 1989 with a coup led by Charles Taylor. Fighting escalated as different factions formed their own armies, some using children. War ended in 1993.
Mozambique	Conflict and civil war continued from the 1960s until elections in 1994.
Myanmar (Burma)	Resistance from Karens and other ethnic groups was finally crushed by government forces in 1995, but human rights abuses are widespread.
Rwanda/ Burundi/Zaire	War between Hutus and Tutsis threatens to spread through the Great Lakes region.
Sierra Leone	Civil war has continued for some years, with foreign mercenary forces fighting on the government side.
Sri Lanka	Civil war has raged since 1983 between Hindu Tamils and Buddhist Sinhalese. The two sides signed a truce in 2002.
Sudan	War between northern Muslim Arabs and southern Sudanese has been going on since the mid-1950s. The war reached new levels of violence in the 1990s.
Turkey	War between government forces and Kurdish nationalists has been going on for years.
The former Yugoslavia	In the 1990s, there were wars of independence within and between breakaway states.

Economic Pressures

When people feel that there is little chance of improving their lives in their own country, it is natural for them to seek a better life somewhere else. This phenomenon is not new. People have been moving in search of a better life throughout history. Whenever a poor country is situated next to a rich country, people from the poor country are naturally interested in moving to the rich country. The migrants hope that they will find jobs in the rich country.

Such a border lies between the United States and Mexico. Mexicans, along with people from other countries south of the border, seek jobs and better living conditions in the United States. Sometimes, they lack the kind of qualifications they need to find good jobs in the U.S. This leaves them with low-paying jobs—performing janitorial, construction, or retail work. In some cases, their standard of living does improve, and they are able to send money home to support close or extended family members.

The U.S., however, does not have an open door policy for immigrants. The U.S. receives approximately one

---

It is natural for people to migrate in search of a better life.

---

million immigrants annually, with 200,000 to 300,000 people entering illegally. People who are granted citizenship have to be included in social programs such as employment and health benefits, which strains resources. On the other hand, every new legal citizen is another taxpayer, and statistics show that most immigrants live healthier lives than average U.S. citizens. This means that more taxes are put into the system and fewer health care benefits leave the system.

Immigrants also provide the labor many countries need in order to grow, and this is a pattern that has existed for centuries. Thousands of Irish people immigrated to Great Britain and the United States in the 19th and 20th centuries.

▬ **Many people do not believe they can improve their living conditions in their own countries. In order to reduce the economic pressure to migrate, international agencies help poor nations develop work programs for women and other underprivileged groups.**

FROM RAGS TO RICHES

On average, people in **developing countries** make much less money than people in developed countries. These higher incomes make rich countries attractive to people in developing countries. The World Bank reports that there are currently about 58 low-income countries with populations of one million or more. Their combined population is almost 3.5 billion. Migration of these people will continue until the standard of living improves in these developing countries.

Low-income and middle-income economies

High-income economies

This large force of laborers helped drive the Industrial Revolution by building canals, railways, and buildings.

The rights of immigrants differ from country to country. In Great Britain, Irish migrants were given voting rights and could bring their families with them. Germany did not give its Polish and Italian immigrants the same privileges, even though these people helped industrialize the country. Switzerland has also relied heavily on its immigrants, but it makes the citizenship process difficult for them.

Nineteenth-century Australia was a vast open country with great potential for development. It needed immigrants for this development. For nearly 100 years, the Australian government tried to fill Australia with people from North America and Europe, but since 1973, the country has taken immigrants from all countries, making Australia one of the most multicultural countries in the world. The society has been transformed, and the economy is dynamic.

The countries of the Middle East employ immigrants to work in the oil industry, but many of these immigrants have no civil rights, live in almost prison-like conditions, and experience harsh treatment. Still, these immigrants may make more money than they would at home. This allows them to send money home to their families. There are many cases where the **gross national product** (GNP) of a country is largely based on money coming from its citizens working in other countries. For example,

Remittances represent the second-largest international flow of money. Many people who work outside their countries in order to support their families, especially women and children, endure harsh working conditions.

25 percent of Jordon's GNP comes from money sent home by its citizens working in other countries.

Money sent home is called **remittance**, and worldwide remittances total about $75 billion each year. This arrangement of foreign workers sending money home is good for the economies of both countries. These remittances will often decline, however, once a worker settles into a country permanently and begins to incur expenses that are common for a permanent resident. This is why many governments make the process of becoming a permanent resident difficult for immigrant workers.

If immigrant workers do not become permanent residents, the host country will not have to worry about caring for them, and the home country can expect a great deal of money to come home during these short-term contracts.

The need for foreign workers does not stay at the same level year after year. In the United States, years of high unemployment are not good years for the country to receive immigrants. If there are no jobs for new citizens, they will need to be supported. High unemployment in the U.S. does not stop people in developing countries from migrating, and the **illegal immigrant** trade helps to get some people into the United States.

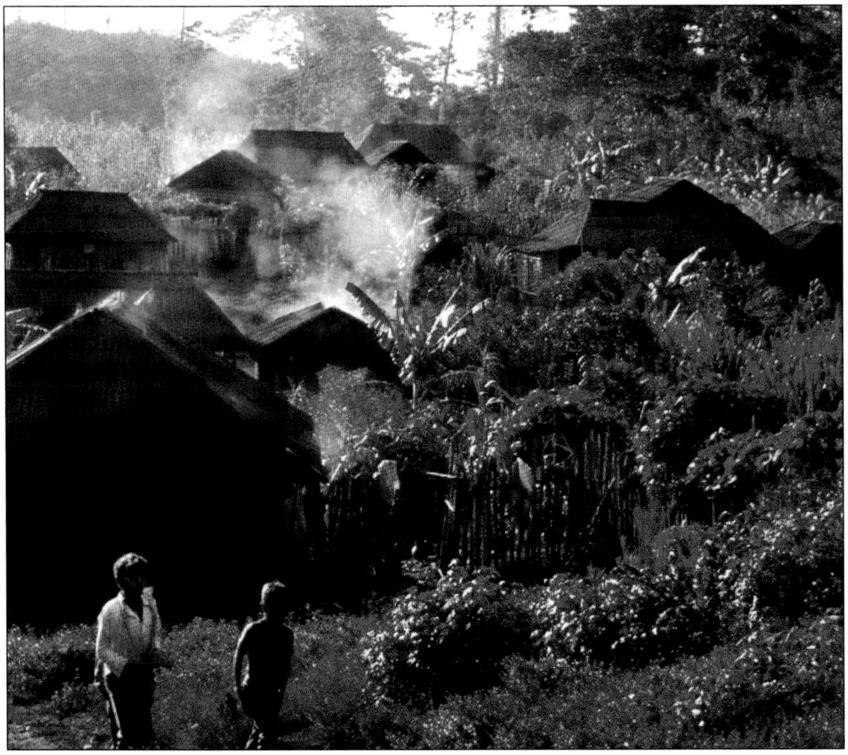

Many people from Latin America immigrate to the United States in hopes of finding better living conditions and more economic opportunities. In 2000, there were more than 32 million Hispanic people living in the United States.

HOW FAST IS THE U.S. HISPANIC POPULATION GROWING?

The Hispanic population in the U.S. is increasing rapidly, and it is expected to be the second fastest-growing population, after Asians, over the next several years. Much of this growth is due to immigration, legal or illegal. Also, the birth rate for Hispanics is 50 percent greater than the national average. In 2000, the number of Hispanic people in the U.S. was well under 50 million. By 2050, the number of Hispanic people living in the U.S. is expected to be about 100 million.

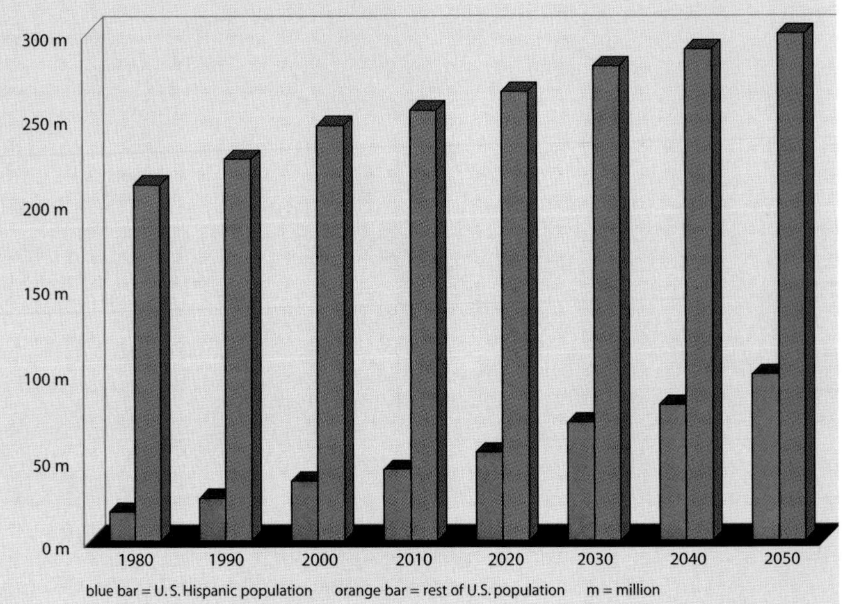
300 m
250 m
200 m
150 m
100 m
50 m
0 m
1980
1990
2000
2010
2020
2030
2040
2050
blue bar = U.S. Hispanic population
orange bar = rest of U.S. population
m = million

MOBILITY OF LABOR AND CONTROLLING IMMIGRATION

The ease of modern travel and the widening gap between rich and poor nations have increased the flow of economic immigrants around the world. Economic immigrants include those who have few resources and migrate to developed countries in search of a better quality of life. Professionals, such as doctors, lawyers, and engineers, from developing countries also migrate to technologically developed nations in search of higher wages, more recognition, and more opportunity for professional development.

Economic migrants are often important to the development of a country. For example, approximately 70 percent of the labor force in Saudi Arabia are migrant workers. Without these migrant workers, Saudi Arabia would find it difficult to maintain its oil industry. Other countries that depend on migrant labor include Australia, Bahrain, Canada, France, Germany, Jordan, Kuwait, Malaysia, Qatar, Russia, Singapore, the Ukraine, United Arab Emirates, and the United States.

Countries such as Great Britain are experiencing a shortage of skilled workers and have made it easier to enter the labor market. Other countries, such as Singapore, have strict controls on immigration. In Singapore, technical and professional people are welcomed, and many unskilled workers from Malaysia, Thailand, Indonesia, and the Philippines work on short-term contracts. Contract workers cannot bring their families with them, and they are not allowed to marry Singaporean nationals. Female immigrants who become pregnant are sent home. Illegal immigrants face three months in jail and three strokes of the cane.

Economic migrants face many hardships. The challenge for countries that need these workers to fuel their economies is to balance the human rights of migrant workers and the need to maintain social stability.

The Attraction of a Better Standard of Living–GDP per Person in U.S. Currency (2000)

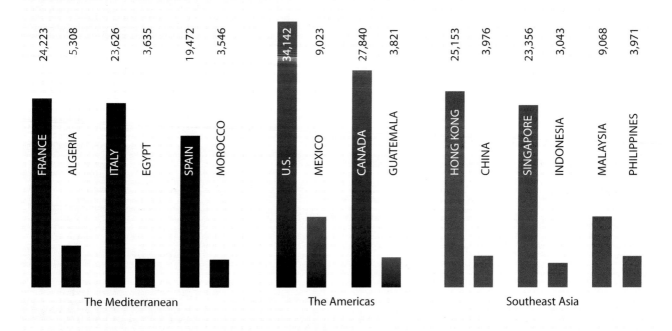

The Mediterranean						The Americas				Southeast Asia					
FRANCE	ALGERIA	ITALY	EGYPT	SPAIN	MOROCCO	U.S.	MEXICO	CANADA	GUATEMALA	HONG KONG	CHINA	SINGAPORE	INDONESIA	MALAYSIA	PHILIPPINES
24,223	5,308	23,626	3,635	19,472	3,546	34,142	9,023	27,840	3,821	25,153	3,976	23,356	3,043	9,068	3,971

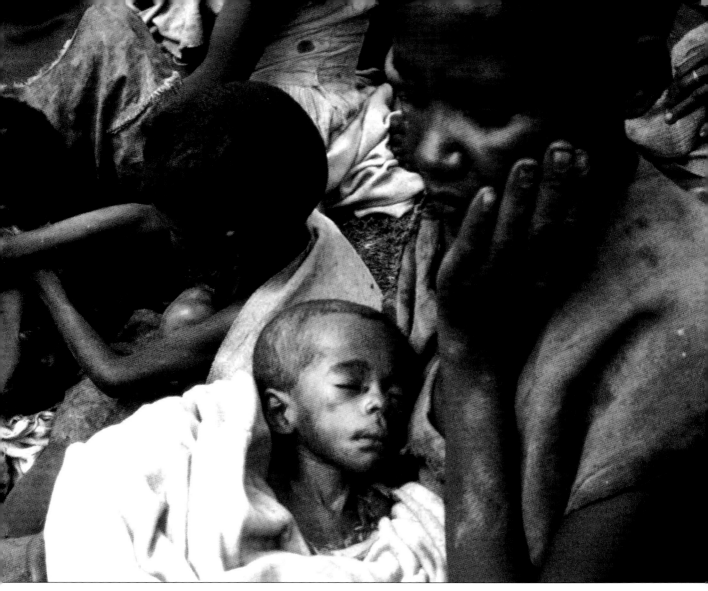

▨▨▨ The World Bank reports that there were 44 countries with severe debt in 2002. People in these countries live in extreme poverty.

KEY CONCEPTS

Industrial Revolution The Industrial Revolution began in England in the 1700s. Manufacturers started using machines to produce items traditionally made by hand. Cotton fabric was one of the first industrially produced goods. As the Industrial Revolution spread to the United States and European countries, it changed the economies of these countries. Traditionally, people had worked at home. They usually made or grew their own goods to sell. Often, they were paid to make goods for larger businesses to sell. After the Industrial Revolution, workers worked on machines in factories. They were usually paid very low wages and worked long hours in dangerous conditions.

World Bank The World Bank helps developing countries fight poverty and establish economic growth that is stable, sustainable, and equitable. The World Bank offers a wide range of services to support the development and implementation of poverty-reduction activities in its member countries.

English as a Second Language (ESL) Teacher

Duties: Creates and delivers lesson plans and activities to help immigrants learn English. Helps integrate newcomers into North American society.

Education: Bachelor's degree in education; a second language would be helpful

Interests: Education, languages, helping others

Navigate to the Web site **www. eflweb.com** for more information about a career as an English as a Second Language (ESL) teacher. Also click on **www-writing. berkeley. edu/TESL-EJ/ej22/a1.html** to learn more about teaching English as a second language.

Careers in Focus

English as a Second Language (ESL) teachers perform many of the same functions as teachers of other languages. An ESL teacher teaches people who are new to North America. In fact, ESL teachers do more than teach the English language. They introduce the culture of North America to people from different countries.

The whole process of leaving one's country can be overwhelming, and ESL teachers help newcomers feel welcome and comfortable in their new home. They help immigrants find new opportunities and make migration a positive experience.

Teaching life skills is a big part of an ESL teacher's duties. Newcomers need to know how to buy groceries, how U.S. currency works, how to get a bank account, and how to ask for help. They need to know where they can look for a job, how to help their children with school, and where to live. This is much more than teaching a language.

ESL teachers have careers that truly give back. An ESL teacher learns bits of other languages and is introduced to the cultures, religious practices, holidays, and food of newcomers. ESL teachers are human specialists.

Politics, Ethnicity, Religion

While globalization is rapidly removing barriers and bringing the world closer together, there are still many different cultures in the world. In some cases, these cultural differences are considered a source of strength, but in many other cases, they are viewed as a source of tension and violence. There are still many cases where violence is used to force a way of life on people. Sometimes this violence involves religion. Other times it involves one political group trying to gain power. However, in almost all of these situations, refugees are the result, and the world's humanitarian organizations are called on to help.

The countries of Africa, Asia, and the Middle East have the world's greatest number of refugees and displaced people, with 8.8 million in Asia alone. More than three million Palestinian refugees live in 59 UN-operated refugee camps in the areas surrounding Israel.

Ethnic differences are seen as a strength in some countries. There are times, however, when ethnic differences cause tensions. These tensions sometimes erupt into armed conflicts. Religious differences have also been the cause of many conflicts around the world.

Since the War on Terrorism in 2001, almost two million Afghan refugees have returned home. However, because of

---

In many cases, violence is used to force a way of life on people.

---

continued instability and drought, there are still 3.6 million Afghan refugees living in Pakistan and Iran. Also, there are several million Kurds living as refugees in northern Iraq or in the mountains of Turkey and Iran. Many of these refugee situations have existed for several years.

While developed countries have become concerned about the number of refugees who want to immigrate, the amount of assistance from countries of the Muslim world is impressive. Iran and Pakistan have given shelter to more than five million refugees in recent years, mainly from war-torn Afghanistan. This number has increased since the War on Terrorism.

YUGOSLAVIA

As the Yugoslavian federation broke apart, the people of Croatia and Slovenia renewed a 50-year-old conflict with Serbia. The war in Croatia led to hundreds of thousands of refugees. Bosnia also declared independence, but Serbians living there wished to remain in the Federation of Yugoslavia. This led to the **ethnic cleansing** of Bosnian Muslims and a takeover of Bosnia by Serb forces. Even after the creation of Bosnia-Herzegovina, the war did not stop. In 1995, Croatian military campaigns resulted in the mass exodus of about 200,000 Serbs from Croatia.

In 1998, about 90 percent of the people living in Kosovo were Muslim Albanian. The government of Kosovo, however, was Christian Serbian. That year, a Kosovo Liberation group announced its plan to split from Yugoslavia and become part of Albania. The Serbian government retaliated, creating more than 850,000 Muslim Albanian refugees who fled to Albania, Macedonia, and other nearby countries. In 1999, Serbian troops pulled out of Kosovo. Albanian refugees returned slowly, but often, they returned to lost homes, land mines, and racial tension. Serbians, fearing violent conflict with returning Albanians, began to flee the area.

Refugee camps are difficult places in which to live. People are cramped together in housing that is meant to be temporary. Some children grow up angry, and they resent the people responsible for their family situation. In this way, a refugee camp is the perfect breeding ground for extremist groups, and angry youths are being used to fight the governments that created the refugee situations. Therefore, refugee camps can create instability in the countries where they exist.

The organized transfer of entire populations by government decree is rare, but there are some examples. During the 1930s and 1940s in Russia, Joseph Stalin, Premier of the former Soviet Union from 1929 to 1953, uprooted hundreds of thousands of Chechens, Tartars, Estonians, Latvians, and other ethnic groups. They were sent to remote parts of the Soviet Union. During China's cultural revolution, from 1966 to 1976, Mao Tse-tung, Chairman of the Chinese Communist Party from 1949 to 1975, sent millions of educated Chinese to work in the countryside. Since 1950, Indonesia has moved as many as 6.5 million people from Java to other islands in an effort to reduce overcrowding.

Large-scale migration has been seen as a good way to colonize areas and gain power. As the world's population increased, it was clear that land was power because with land comes space and resources. The British increased their empire by sending thousands of people to colonize North America and Australia. In fact, every major empire practiced colonization. The French claimed much of North America; the Spanish conquered the lands of South America; and many nations claimed countries in Africa.

Many other migrations happened as a result of the breakup of countries or other major events. The collapse of the Soviet Union in the early 1990s led to a large movement of people. The Soviets united many countries under one flag. When the state collapsed, these countries regained their individual identity, and 50 million people suddenly found themselves in foreign countries. Central Asia saw intertribal violence and mass migrations during this collapse. Borders had been drawn without considering these groups, and once the Soviet Union collapsed, borders had to find their own natural order.

After the end of the Cold War, which lasted from 1945 to 1990, millions of Jewish people left the former Soviet

KEY CONCEPTS

Cold War The Cold War between the U.S. and the Soviet Union lasted from 1945 to 1990. Although there was never any actual fighting, a war still occurred. In this case, the war was fought with words. The two most powerful nations on the planet, the U.S. and Soviet Union, were arguing over which type of government and society was the best. The U.S. has always been a **democracy**, with a strong capitalist base. A **capitalist system** is based on the belief that private citizens have the right to own businesses and earn money on their own merit. The Soviet Union was a communist society. A **communist system** is based on the idea that all factories and production are controlled by the government. The government then distributes the wealth evenly among its citizens so that poverty is eliminated.

Colonization Colonization occurs when a state has political and economic control over an area occupied by a native population that does not have the same organizational or technological influence. Colonization can involve a migration of nationals to the territory, or it may be formal control over the territory by military or civil representatives of the dominant power. Colonization can take the form of state policy, or it may be a private project sponsored by chartered corporations or by associations and individuals.

Union. About half of them went to Israel, which gives automatic citizenship to all Jewish people under the Law of Return. This huge influx of people has had many consequences. There was a need to build and restructure the country. Much of this work has been done by more than 200,000 foreign workers. Many of these workers are illegal immigrants, and they live in poor conditions. Some Israelis argue that foreign workers should be expelled to preserve the Jewish nature of the state.

Conditions in refugee camps can be terrible. Refugees may be forced to live in mud and straw huts or under pieces of plastic.

KURDS

The Kurds, a group of 20 million non-Arab people, are the largest ethnic group without a state of their own. The area they claim as Kurdistan lies at the mountainous intersection of Iraq, Iran, Turkey, and Syria. The Kurds were promised this home state in the Treaty of Sèvres following World War I, but the treaty was renegotiated later to exclude this state. Kurds are a very diverse group, with many religions, languages, cultures, and political agendas. After the 1991 Gulf War, a Kurdish uprising was crushed by Iraqi forces. Nearly 500,000 Kurds fled to the Iraq-Turkey border, and another one million fled to Iran. These refugees created a serious humanitarian crisis. Since the end of the Gulf War, the Kurds have lived in northern Iraq, protected by a "no-fly zone" created by the international community.

Mapping People on the Move

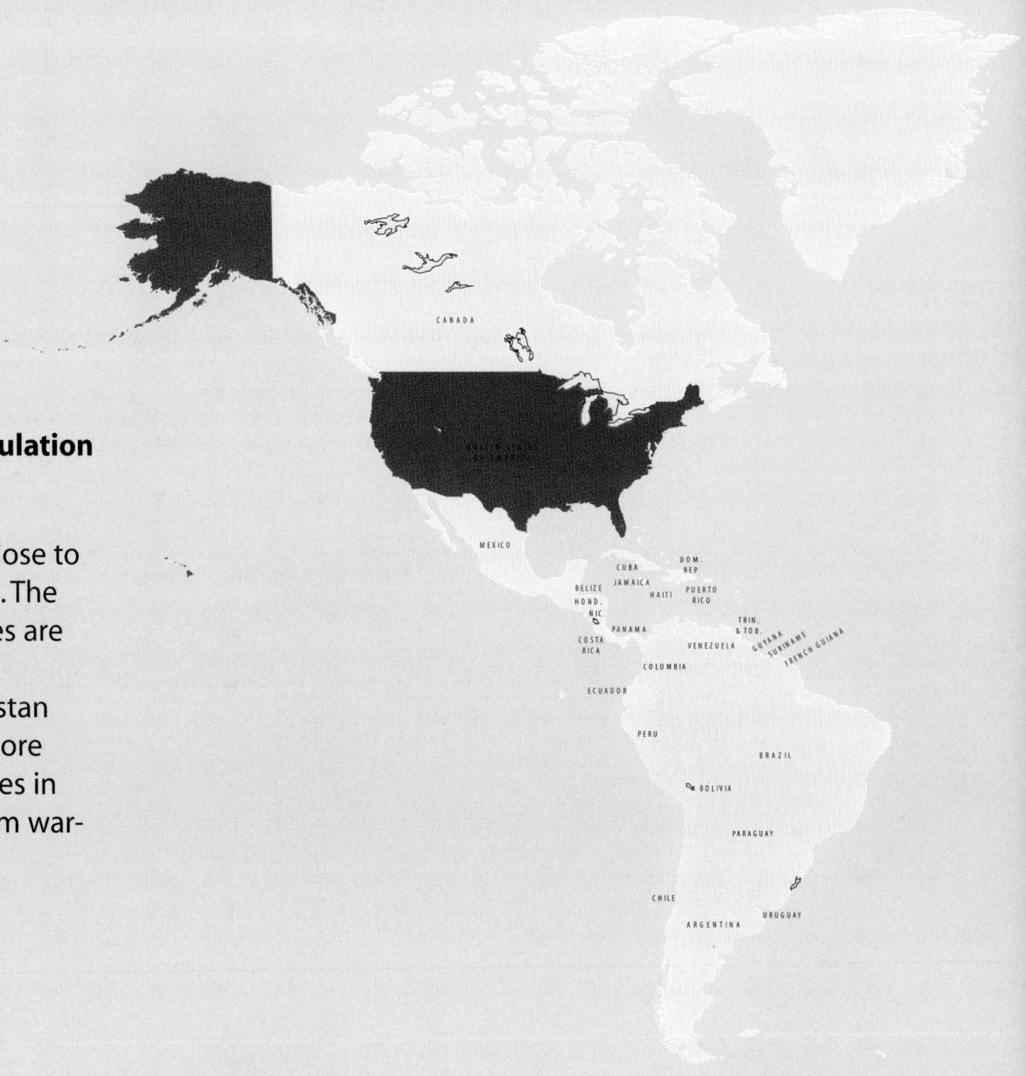

Figure 1: Refugee Population by Host Country

Most refugees stay as close to their homes as possible. The vast majority of refugees are hosted by developing countries. Iran and Pakistan have given shelter to more than five million refugees in recent years, mainly from war-torn Afghanistan.

	0–49,999
	50,000–74,999
	75,000–249,999
	250,000–499,999
	500,000–999,999
	more than 1,000,000

CANADA

UNITED STATES OF AMERICA

MEXICO

BELIZE
GUATEMALA
HOND.
NIC.
COSTA RICA
PANAMA

CUBA
JAMAICA
HAITI
DOM. REP
PUERTO RICO

TRIN. & TOB.
VENEZUELA
GUYANA
SURINAME
FRENCH GUIANA

COLOMBIA
ECUADOR
PERU
BOLIVIA
BRAZIL
PARAGUAY
CHILE
URUGUAY
ARGENTINA

Scale 1:101,080,000

Charting the World's Migrants

Figure 2: Global Refugees and Others of Concern to the United Nations High Commissioner for Refugees

The UNHCR is responsible for people who have been forced to leave their homes because of war, persecution, and natural disaster.

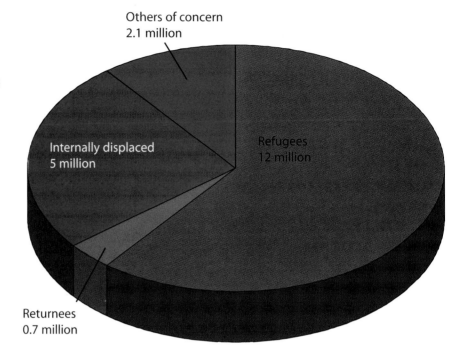

Others of concern
2.1 million

Internally displaced
5 million

Refugees
12 million

Returnees
0.7 million

Figure 3: Number of Refugees by Region

Most refugees live in regions that cannot afford to care for them.

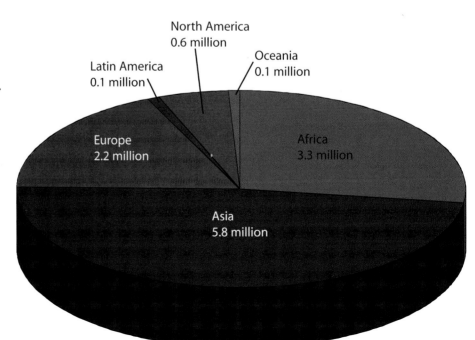

North America
0.6 million

Oceania
0.1 million

Latin America
0.1 million

Europe
2.2 million

Africa
3.3 million

Asia
5.8 million

Figure 4: Top Ten Internally Displaced Populations

Not all refugees move to other countries. Some stay in their own country.

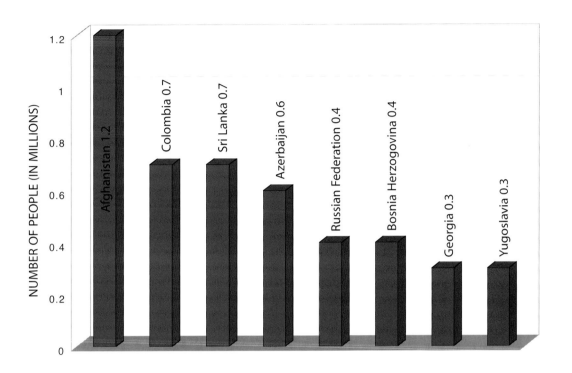

NUMBER OF PEOPLE (IN MILLIONS)

Afghanistan 1.2
Colombia 0.7
Sri Lanka 0.7
Azerbaijan 0.6
Russian Federation 0.4
Bosnia Herzogovina 0.4
Georgia 0.3
Yugoslavia 0.3

Figure 5: Growth of Global Refugee Population

The number of refugees has grown dramatically since 1975.

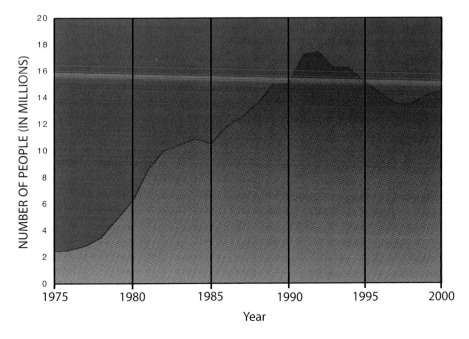

NUMBER OF PEOPLE (IN MILLIONS)

Year

Natural and Man-Made Disasters

Floods, fires, volcanic eruptions, avalanches, mudslides, and storms have all been a regular part of the history of the planet. When natural disasters affect people, the most common response is to move away from that area.

The number of migrants created by natural disasters is small when compared to the number of migrants created by war, persecution, or economic pressures. However, the number of these disasters seems to be increasing. Some of the extreme weather is due to **global warming**, and many people feel that global warming is caused by human activity. As time goes by, global warming could create more of the natural disasters that cause people to migrate.

Of all natural disasters, earthquakes pose the greatest danger to human life. In 1976, the Tang Shan earthquake in China killed more than 500,000 people. Earthquakes occur suddenly and cause terrible and immediate destruction. Although an earthquake may not be responsible for a large number of refugees or migrants, it does force many people out of their homes and communities. These displaced people will need aid from governments and nongovernmental organizations to start again.

Other forms of natural disasters, such as fires, floods, and storms, lead to more refugees because they occur after people have been warned. This gives people time to leave their homes and move somewhere safe. Fires, floods, and storms do not happen instantly, but their range of destruction can be large and long-lasting. These types of disasters can leave large numbers of people without homes, and in the case of fires and floods, many people may not be able to return to their original homes or communities.

Lack of food or resources can be considered a natural disaster as well. If widespread crop loss occurs, sometimes people must move in search of food.

Overcrowding due to an increase in population can also degrade the environment and limit the available food supply. This man-made disaster has caused mass migration in countries such as Brazil and Uzbekistan.

Populations in many parts of Africa are growing too quickly, and drought is a regular but unpredictable event. When there are more people than food to feed them, mass starvation occurs.

According to statistics compiled during the United Nations International Decade for Natural Disaster Reduction, natural disasters leave millions of people homeless each year.

EARTHQUAKE, FLOOD, AND STORM

Populous areas close to sea level or near large rivers are susceptible to flooding. Floods can leave thousands of people homeless within a single day. Powerful floods swept across Europe in 2002, resulting in approximately 100 deaths and thousands of refugees. Prague, in the Czech Republic, saw its worst flood in 200 years as the raging river Vltava reached its crest. In the end, more than 200,000 people were evacuated from their homes, many houses were destroyed, and the cost of damages was estimated at $3 billion.

This was the case in Ethiopia, Somalia, and other countries. Images of starvation, famine, and disease were signs that there were more people than could be maintained by the available resources.

Acquired immunodeficiency syndrome (AIDS), a disease of the human immune system, also has had a major impact on Africa, leaving large numbers of children homeless every year. Left hungry and alone, they join the migrating masses.

Government projects that require or affect large spaces of land can also cause migration. The Three Gorges project in China will result in the world's largest dam and hydroelectric power plant. The huge lake created by the dam is expected to drive more than one million people from their homes. The Three Gorges Reservoir will also put 76,603 acres (31,000 ha) of farmland underwater and will require the relocation of 1,599 industrial and mining enterprises, as well as power

lines and roads. Globally, more than 10 million people have to leave their homes every year because of an energy or transportation project.

Some human projects unexpectedly lead to a rise in refugees. The Chernobyl nuclear power plant explosion in 1986 led to the evacuation of more than 100,000 people. Ever since, people have been leaving the general area fearing contamination and associated health risks.

HURRICANE FLOYD

With such a large land area, the United States can experience floods, droughts, tropical storms, and snowstorms, all within the same year. Hurricane Floyd, a tropical storm, struck the mid-Atlantic coast of the U.S. in 1999. Forty-nine deaths have now been attributed to the storm, which dumped torrential rain from the Carolinas to New Jersey and produced record flooding in eastern North Carolina. Hurricane Floyd caused more than $6 billion worth of damage.

KEY CONCEPTS

Chernobyl In the early hours of April 26, 1986, workers at the nuclear power plant in Chernobyl began a shutdown procedure. Twenty seconds later, a power surge created a chemical explosion so powerful it blew the cover off the top of the reactor. A faulty cooling system was partially at fault, but human error was largely to blame. The accident that destroyed the reactor in Unit Four killed 31 people immediately, and radioactive material spewed over the surrounding countryside. As a result, birth defects have become a long-term reality in the lands nearby, including Belarus and Ukraine. Unit Four is now encased in concrete and steel, which is showing signs of weakening.

Three Gorges China has used the Yangtze River as its central highway for countless centuries. It is 3,700 miles (5,955 km) long and runs through the center of the country. Millions of people

■■■■■ **After the Chernobyl nuclear power plant explosion, 210,000 people were forced to move to less contaminated areas.**

live along its banks. They use the river to transport people and goods and to obtain water for their farmlands. In 1989, the government decided to use the river for a large dam/power plant project. At the chosen location, the river runs through three large gorges at the foot of several mountains. It is estimated that building the dam will cost more than $24 billion. Work on the giant project began in 1994 and is scheduled to be finished in 2016. Chinese officials claim the dam will control the unpredictable Yangtze River, which frequently floods and kills thousands of people. The dam will also provide China with one-ninth of its present power needs. In the process of damming the river, 140 towns and 300 villages will be put underwater, including many historical sites. This project will force 1.2 million people to resettle before its completion.

Trafficking in Migrants

In 2001, CNN reported that an estimated 50,000 women and children are smuggled into the United States every year. The victims, often from Asia and the former Soviet republics, believe they are going to the U.S. to work in a legitimate job. Instead, they are forced to be prostitutes or nude dancers.

This is not just a U.S. problem. Many countries are suppliers and receivers of illegal immigrants. As many as 700,000 to 1,000,000 people are living as immigrant slaves worldwide.

In 1997, it was estimated that organized crime was making $7 billion a year moving immigrants illegally from country to country. Human trafficking is a fast-growing

---

Trafficking in migrants is a $7 billion a year industry.

---

industry, and so are the profits for crime lords. Many of the people who seek a new life in a new country do not have the necessary paperwork, such as passports or citizenship papers. Some of these people are prepared to spend all of their savings to get to these new lands.

There are some genuine organizations that deal with the paperwork and transport of legal migrants, but there are many more illegal organizations, backed by gangs, performing similar functions. Many of these illegal organizations transport immigrants in terrible conditions. Many take the money of immigrants and leave them drifting at sea. Some coerce immigrants into a world of crime once they arrive at their destination. Some organizations simply drop the immigrants off in the new, strange land without money or living arrangements.

Still, there is such a high demand for safe passage from

There are approximately 3.3 million refugees in Africa. These people have been forced to flee from their homes by civil war and ethnic violence.

poor countries to rich countries that a multi-billion-dollar industry has been formed. Unfortunately, some immigrants are criminals, and in a new country, they may quickly form gangs or drug rings. Most immigrants, however, are not criminals. Instead, they may be migrating to escape a state of lawlessness that is disrupting their homeland. This is true of the former Yugoslavia, Russia, and the countries of Central Asia.

Migrants often come from developing countries. The destination for immigrants from these countries is most often the developed countries of Europe or North America. The countries that were once a source of migrants, such as Italy, Greece, and Spain, have now become a major target for immigrants. Laws of migration for these countries are often so loose that these countries receive more immigrants than they can handle. Italy is a favored landing point for immigrants. The Mafia charges $600 per person for the boat ride from North Africa to Sicily, an island off the coast of mainland Italy. In the U.S., the border with Mexico is the main crossover point for illegal immigrants. It is a long border and difficult to police.

Sometimes, the goal of parents is to find their children a home where they will be healthier, happier, and have a better chance of survival. In this case, the migrants are children. There are many countries and organizations that want children, and some of them are better than others. Westerners, eager to adopt a child, sometimes buy children from various countries, including Romania and Mexico.

The problem of buying children is just as bad, or worse, in other countries. Brothel owners in India buy thousands of Nepalese girls every year.

More than half the world's refugees are children. Many of these children are subjected to violence and exploitation. Sometimes they are forced to become soldiers or slaves.

MIGRATING BY FORCE OR BY CHOICE

People will move out of hope, fear, or by force. Neither African Americans nor European Americans are native to North America. In general, Europeans came to United States out of hope for a better life. African Americans were taken by force from their homes in Africa. This was not seen as trafficking because it was legal to sell and own slaves at the time. Slavery is no longer legal under international law.

These girls find themselves in conditions of virtual slavery. The city of Bombay has 50,000 Nepalese girls working in its brothels at any one time. Government does little to end this trade, but organizations such as United Nations Children's Fund (UNICEF) work to prevent and end these situations.

The trade in women is large. Women from Thailand, Brazil, the Philippines, and the Dominican Republic are recruited for prostitution. Many women are lured to the U.S. with tales of guaranteed jobs. Once they are in the U.S., they find that they are the property of the people who transported them, and they must work in the sex trade. In the end, these women may become more entwined in crime as they are often expected to carry or sell drugs.

The International Organization for Migration (IOM) reports that since 1998, between 700,000 and 2,000,000 women and children were being smuggled annually. IOM admits that these figures are hard to confirm because trafficking is so secretive. In 2000, IOM helped 703 victims return to their homes voluntarily, and it was able to gather valuable information about human trafficking from these victims. Most of these victims were women or children who came from Moldova, Romania, the Ukraine, and Cambodia.

Africa also has a major problem with the trafficking of women and children. The government of Nigeria reported

It is often difficult to protect children who are refugees. Many international agencies and the United Nations High Commissioner for Refugees are working to overcome the political, logistical, and financial challenges of protecting these vulnerable children.

that 1,178 women and children were victims of trafficking between March 1999 and December 2000. IOM has worked to **repatriate** 2,000 children from Mali who have been forced to work on plantations as servants and prostitutes.

Migrant trafficking has always been a human rights issue, but when it involves children, the public becomes especially outraged. The President of Nigeria states that child labor and the trafficking of women are similar to the slave trade of the 18th and 19th centuries and that these practices must be eliminated.

Other instances of migrants being mistreated are harder to punish. Many migrants are not actually abducted and forced to work. Instead, they willingly go to jobs that pay them very little. Thousands of people, especially women, suffer abuse and work for as little as $100 a month. Although this may be an improvement over extreme poverty and starvation, these people are being exploited in the very countries where they are seeking help.

Desperate migrants are being exploited by people who have something the migrants need—money, food, shelter, or transportation. Perhaps the only way to stop the crime of human trafficking is to help the desperate thousands legally acquire those things they need.

PROVIDING HUMANITARIAN AID

Providing aid for refugees has become the joint responsibility of governments, multinational agencies, and private organizations. UNICEF, United Nations High Commissioner for Refugees (UNHCR), Red Cross/Red Crescent, Oxfam, and USAID are all examples of these types of organizations.

The most basic needs of humans are food, water, and shelter. These are the first factors considered when dealing with refugee crises. Shelters may consist of huts, tents, or simple plastic sheeting draped for cover. Food is more complicated. Most aid groups distribute food in terms of daily requirements for healthy individuals.

Distribution is a complicated process. While it is common and acceptable for people to trade their food for clothes or fuel, it is not acceptable for food to be stolen. As food is the only source of wealth in a refugee camp, it is often hoarded by gangs looking to make a profit. To reduce the chance of raw food being stolen, kitchens are often set up to distribute cooked food to people. Ration cards are also used to keep a close watch on who is getting the food. Plastic ration cards that work with computer terminals can solve problems associated with paper ration cards.

Managed distribution, however, is not possible in cases where food is airdropped into combat zones. In these cases, hoarding is unavoidable, and many people will continue to go hungry.

As well, refugee leaders may misreport their numbers in order to make profits by selling extra food. In Somalia, 300,000 people registered for aid, although the actual number in need of aid was closer to 170,000.

This kind of corruption makes complicated systems of distribution necessary. The large number of workers needed to make these systems work puts a larger burden on humanitarian agencies that are trying to put as much money toward food as they can.

UNHCR's primary purpose is to protect the rights and well-being of refugees. It also seeks to provide a minimum of food, water, shelter, and medical care for refugees worldwide.

KEY CONCEPTS

International law International law is a group of rules and principles that countries are expected to follow, despite each country's own separate laws. International law ensures countries deal with one another effectively. International law especially applies to wars. Rules such as those for conduct in war are often formed during international conventions. Refugees have special rights under international law.

The International Organization for Migration (IOM) IOM is an intergovernmental body that has 59 member states and 42 observer states. Its goal is to ensure the orderly migration of people in need of international assistance. IOM works to prevent the illegal trafficking of immigrants. It helps illegal immigrants, asylum seekers who have been rejected, students who are stranded, and others return home. In emergency situations, IOM stabilizes populations by providing emergency relief and short-term community development programs.

UNHCR The United Nations High Commissioner for Refugees was founded in 1951 to help the refugees of World War II. UNHCR still provides protection for refugees. Over the years, the organization has expanded to serve not only refugees, but also internally displaced people and those fleeing disasters. Operations for this branch of the UN cost more than $1 billion per year. Most of this money comes from donations from the wealthier member nations of the UN.

UNICEF UNICEF was founded in 1946 as the United Nations International Children's Emergency Fund. Since 1953, it has been called the United Nations Children's Fund. The Fund was originally established to meet the emergency needs of children in post-war Europe and China, but its goals were widened to address the long-term needs of children and mothers in developing countries everywhere. UNICEF operates programs in 160 countries, helping "every child reach their full potential through long term and emergency work on health care, education and protection for children at risk."

Duties: Teaches school, provides medical treatment
Education: Various, but expertise in helping children is an asset; medical, educational, and political backgrounds are especially helpful
Interests: Political advocacy, helping people

Navigate to the Web site **www.unicef.org** for more information about careers with UNICEF. Also click on **www.unicef. org/about/ timeline. html** to learn about the history of UNICEF.

Careers in Focus

UNICEF is an organization created to help children around the world. It focuses on child health, nutrition, education, and children in especially difficult circumstances and emergencies. UNICEF hires teachers, doctors, nurses, and public relations people who work to better the lives of children.

UNICEF carries out massive immunization programs in order to prevent major child-killing diseases, such as diphtheria, measles, whooping cough, polio, tuberculosis, and tetanus. It teaches mothers about the basic nutritional needs of children. These tasks require a background in both health care and education.

UNICEF believes every child has the right to an education. It develops educational programs to improve school curriculum and facilities and provides training in important skills. UNICEF develops and provides "Edukits" that consist of materials needed to set up a basic classroom.

UNICEF requires advocates, lawyers, and public relations people to help children affected by disaster, sexual abuse, forced labor, and extreme poverty. The protection of girls is an important function of UNICEF.

When wars and natural disasters disrupt communities, UNICEF helps protect the children in these communities by providing emergency health care, food supplements, rehabilitation, education, and counseling, as well as water and sanitation facilities.

Prevention and Cure

Diversity equals strength in so many different ways. In nature, the more diverse the plants and animals in a given area, the healthier those plants and animals will be. Genetically, the more diverse a population is, the better chance it has to survive. Migrating people carry knowledge, experience, traditions, and beliefs that can enrich any area or community into which they move. This can happen only if they are accepted and helped to find a home and a way of living in that society.

Throughout history, many countries have seen the value of migrants, and migrants have received varying degrees of welcome and support in different places at different times. Still, in many places, migrants are considered to be a negative addition to the population. This is due to widespread racism based on outdated and stereotypical beliefs. Wars are still waged to rid Earth of entire groups of people who are considered evil. These ethnic cleansings did not

Many people find it difficult to leave their native land and settle in a country with unfamiliar traditions. While some immigrants adapt quickly to their new homes, other people try to maintain their native cultures.

end with World War II's Holocaust. They continue in different forms all around the world.

The UN has set up many programs to help migrating people. There have been many humanitarian responses to refugee crises in the last several decades, but migration itself continues to grow every year. This movement serves as a sign that troubling situations exist in countries from which people

---

Wealthy countries are making laws to slow down the migration of people. When thousands of people come across a border without jobs or formal education, a huge strain is put on the system.

---

emigrate in great numbers. Persecution, politics, disaster, and a lack of education, jobs, or food are all reasons to move.

As a result of increased immigration, wealthy countries are beginning to make laws to slow down the migration of people. Social systems, such as health care and welfare, are established to protect residents already living in a country. When thousands of people come across a border without jobs or formal

education, a huge strain is put on the system. The system of asylum is abused in some cases, and often, people trying to claim asylum are sent back to their home countries.

The United States had a very generous asylum policy during the Cold War. This was a way of encouraging people to leave the Soviet Union. Once the Cold War ended, there was an explosion of people wanting to **defect**. The only difference was that the reasons for leaving were economic instead of political. By 1994, the U.S. had a backlog of 420,000 asylum applications. They could only hope to let in 10 to 15 percent of the applicants without putting a strain on social systems. Germany is also a major target for migrants looking for asylum. Its acceptance rate has dropped from 29 percent in 1985 to less than 5 percent in the 1990s.

Immigrants are unwelcome in many countries. In most cases, they are seen as a strain on social systems. However, immigrants put more into a system than they take out.

Economic migrants often come from backgrounds where they struggled to make ends meet. In a country where they have better opportunities, immigrants work diligently and contribute billions of dollars in taxes to their new country.

Still, in many cases, there are just too many people trying to cross borders, and some countries resort to military force to turn people away. Actions such as these make the immigration process seem unjust.

In order to slow down the number of people who want to immigrate, it is necessary to reduce the need to migrate. To meet this goal, the best solution is to improve living conditions in the developing world. This would require many things: an end to poverty, education for all, health care for all, proper sanitation, population controls, fair governments, a huge reduction in weapons and militarization, and an end to racism. These are not easy issues to overcome, but they would reduce the tide of people who wish to migrate every year.

Aid will continue to be necessary, and there is a need for political leadership from powerful countries. The international community, represented by the UN, struggles to deal with civil wars, injustice,

TYPICAL AGRICULTURE KIT FOR REFUGEES

In times of famine, the Red Cross provides food to those in need. It also provides agricultural assistance such as seeds and fertilizer. This assistance allows people to recover from the crisis and provide for themselves in the future.

A typical agriculture kit for refugees includes seeds and tools to cultivate the land. Agriculture kits may help to sustain a population, but if the year is not a good one for crops, the same problem exists. If the crops are abundant, the country's population may grow to a level that cannot survive in a year when crops are poor. While it is necessary to help refugees and homeless people as much as possible, many people feel that population controls would reduce the number of homeless people and refugees.

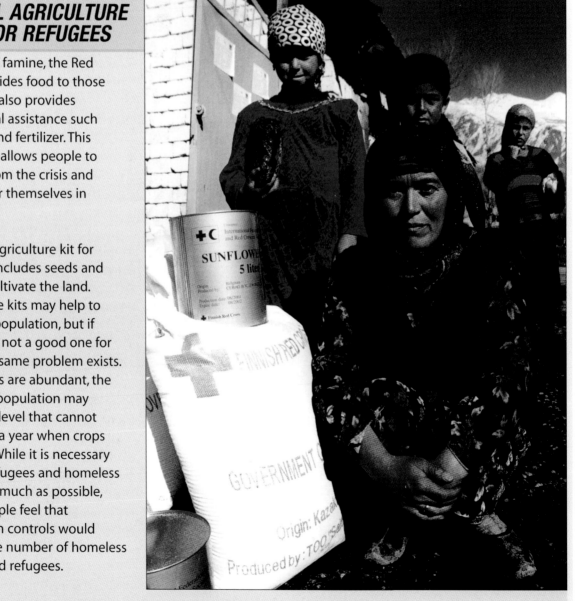

poverty, and refugees. These are concerns that require a large investment in money and workers, but ordinary people can help by donating money, volunteering, or just being tolerant. When every country is safe and offers fair and equal opportunities for its citizens, the number of people migrating will slow down. When racism stops, so will ethnic cleansing. When people's needs are met, civil wars will cease. There will always be natural disasters, and there will always be a need for humanitarian efforts, but human disasters can be prevented with awareness and a sense of global responsibility.

AUSTRALIA'S EFFORTS TO PREVENT ILLEGAL IMMIGRATION

As a result of a surge in illegal immigrants, Australia has been working with other countries and the UN to combat people smuggling. In February 2002, Australia co-chaired with Indonesia the Regional Conference on People Smuggling, Trafficking in Persons and Related Transnational Crime. This conference resulted in an agreement between Australia and its neighbors to work together to fight people smuggling.

Australia is serious about discouraging illegal immigrants from making the long trip to its shores, and it has enacted the Pacific Strategy.

This strategy enables Australia to meet its obligation to protect asylum seekers without allowing them into the country. Under this strategy, the few asylum seekers that reach Australia's shores are held in detention centers until their status is decided. Those who are intercepted at sea have access to refugee status determination processes on Naura, Manus Island (Papua New Guinea), and the Australian territories of Christmas and Cocos Islands.

STEPS TO PREVENTION

Mass migration can cause problems for the host and the recipient countries. The host countries lose their most valuable resource—people. The recipient country has to screen and process newcomers and provide social programs for them. There are many ways to reduce mass migration. One way is to stiffen immigration laws. Another way is to improve conditions in the host country. If conditions improved in the host country, more people would be motivated to stay.

Some countries hold illegal immigrants in detention camps.

Agencies of the United Nations are involved in promoting and maintaining world peace, engage in peacekeeping activities, and offer humanitarian aid to those in need.

KEY CONCEPTS

Asylum The term "asylum" describes the protection from arrest and extradition that is given to refugees by a nation or by an embassy or other agency that has diplomatic immunity. The fundamental problem with the present asylum system is management. Between 1991 and 1995, 2.4 million asylum applications were filed in Western Europe. It is estimated that European countries spent approximately $45 billion managing their asylum systems in the 1990s. In 2001, the cost was $10 billion. Asylum systems were designed to handle small numbers of people. Given the large number of people seeking asylum, developed countries are trying to find a balance between what should be done and what can be done for these people.

United Nations The UN is a group of 191 countries working together to solve global problems. The UN was founded in 1945. The UN's goals are to maintain world peace, develop friendly relations among nations, encourage nations to cooperate in order to solve international problems, and promote respect for human rights.

Born: September 16, 1927, in Tokyo, Japan

Legacy: Expanded the scope of UNHCR to include people who are internally displaced by war, famine, and disaster

Navigate to **www.unhcr. ch/un&ref/ogata/ogata.htm** to learn more about Sadako Ogata. Also click on **www.unhcr.ch** to learn more about the UN High Commissioner for Refugees.

People in Focus

Sadako Ogata was born in Tokyo, Japan, on September 16, 1927. From an early age, she was fascinated by international issues. In addition to a long and distinguished academic career, Ogata has played an important role in international diplomacy.

She has a long-held commitment to humanitarian issues and the ideals of the UN. In 1976, Ogata became the Minister and then Extraordinary Envoy to the Japanese mission to the United Nations. At this time, she also became Chairman of the Executive Board of the UN Children's Fund (UNICEF) and later the Representative of Japan on the UN Commission on Human Rights (UNCHR).

On December 21, 1990, the UN General Assembly elected her to one of the most difficult and crucial jobs on the international humanitarian stage, the High Commissioner for Refugees.

Ogata became the UN High Commissioner for Refugees (UNHCR) on January 1, 1991, and within days, the agency had to decide whether or not it would help more than 400,000 Kurds who were trapped in northern Iraq. The Kurds were unable to leave their country. They were considered displaced persons and fell outside UNHCR's mandate. Ogata decided that UNHCR would assist the Kurds. She said she made this common-sense decision because "the bottom line should always be the welfare and safety of a refugee."

Ogata was UN High Commissioner for Refugees from 1991 to 2000. During this time, UNHCR had to deal with the breakup of the former Yugoslavia, the Rwandan genocide, the Kosovo conflict, and the crisis in Timor. Throughout all these crises, she stressed the need for quick international responses to the urgent needs of the world's displaced people.

Time Line of Events

18,000 B.C.

According to a widely held theory, the first people migrate over the Bering land bridge from Asia to North America. These people later become known as Native Americans.

1771–1775

More than 250,000 Irish and Scottish people migrate to America, mostly due to famine, the failing wool trade, and persecution.

1830

A great flood of migration into North America begins. Most of these people emigrate from Europe.

1845–1850

The Great Potato Famine sends hundreds of thousands of Irish immigrants to the United States.

1914–1918

Millions of people are displaced in Eastern Europe by World War I.

1939–1945

There were approximately one million displaced people in Europe by the end of World War II.

1950–1991

Around 1.5 million people emigrate from the USSR.

1950–1993

Around three million ethnic Germans immigrate to their mother country, most of them from Poland and the USSR.

1956

The war of independence in Algeria unleashes the first major wave of refugees in modern African history as tens of thousands of people flee to Tunisia and Morocco. UNHCR intervenes in 1957, and five years later, it helps repatriate 260,000 Algerians.

1958

After Guinea receives independence from France, one million Guineans are displaced as a result of tensions with the former colonial ruler.

1960

The anti-colonial movement sweeps through central and southern Africa, provoking a widespread movement of people throughout the region.

1962

UNHCR opens its first office in Burundi, Africa, in response to a regional crisis.

1970

There are 2.5 million refugees worldwide.

1975

The UN decides that Western Sahara has the right to self-determination, but war breaks out between Morocco and the Polisario Front. One hundred and fifty thousand refugees from the former British colony of Southern Rhodesia arrive in Mozambique.

1977

War begins in the Horn of Africa, and as many as three million Somalis and Ethiopians are displaced. A year later, UNHCR launches an assistance program for Ethiopian refugees in neighboring countries.

1980

After five violent switches in the Afghan government, the number of Afghan refugees climbs to 600,000.

1983

As war spreads and intensifies, 3.9 million refugees flee from Afghanistan.

1984

The great Ethiopian famine kills hundreds of thousands of people, and many more flee to Sudan, Somalia, and Djibouti.

1988

The Geneva Accords call for the withdrawal of Soviet troops from Afghanistan. While some refugees continue to flee, others begin returning. There are still 5.9 million Afghan refugees.

1989

A UN-brokered political settlement ends South Africa's occupation of Namibia, and 45,000 Namibians return home. Civil war starts in Liberia, and the seven-year-long conflict uproots 700,000 people.

1990

There are 6.2 million Afghan refugees, but 350,000 have returned home since 1988.

1992

There are 18 million refugees worldwide.

1992

A Mozambique peace agreement is signed, and 1.7 million refugees return home in one of the most successful refugee return programs since World War II.

1994

There are 20 million refugees worldwide. There are an estimated 80 million migrants worldwide.

Illegal immigration has been a growing problem since the 1990s, especially for countries with a high standard of living. To combat illegal immigration, some countries have increased security along their borders.

1994

As many as one million people die in Rwanda's genocide, and another 1.7 million people flee the country. Two years later, hundreds of thousands of refugees return to Rwanda, but many thousands die in the rainforests of central Africa.

1997

A military uprising in Sierra Leone starts a cycle of murder and mutilation, and more than 400,000 people flee.

2001

Fighting and drought in Afghanistan spark a new exodus early in the year. After five years with a holding refugee rate of 2.7 million, the number climbs to 3.6 million. Many people are internally displaced as a result of the War on Terrorism. UNHCR establishes the first of 15 new refugee camps in the country's border belt. With the fall of the Taliban in late November, refugees and displaced people begin making their way home.

Concept Web

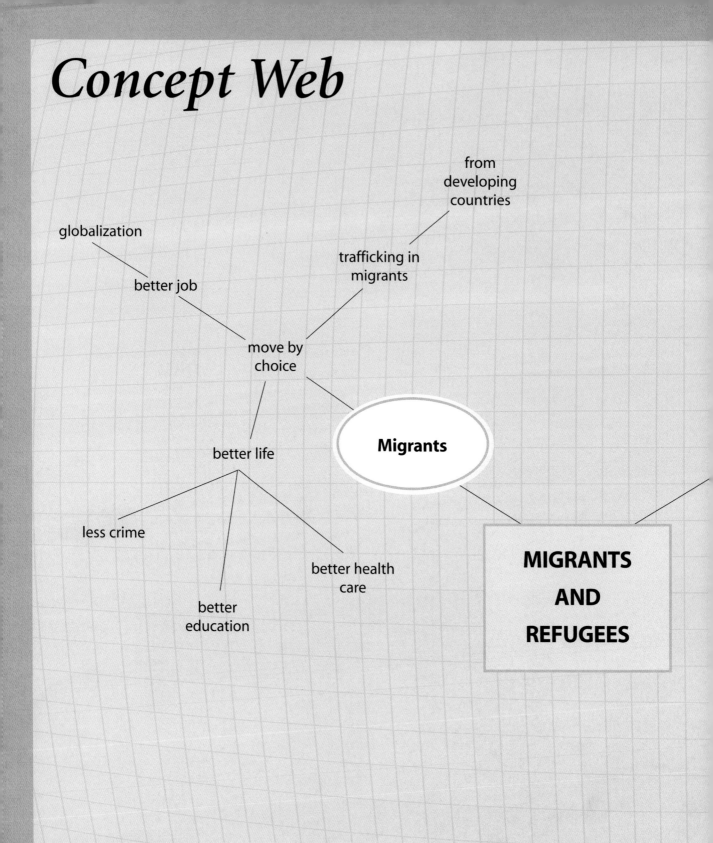

globalization

from developing countries

trafficking in migrants

better job

move by choice

Migrants

better life

less crime

better health care

better education

MIGRANTS AND REFUGEES

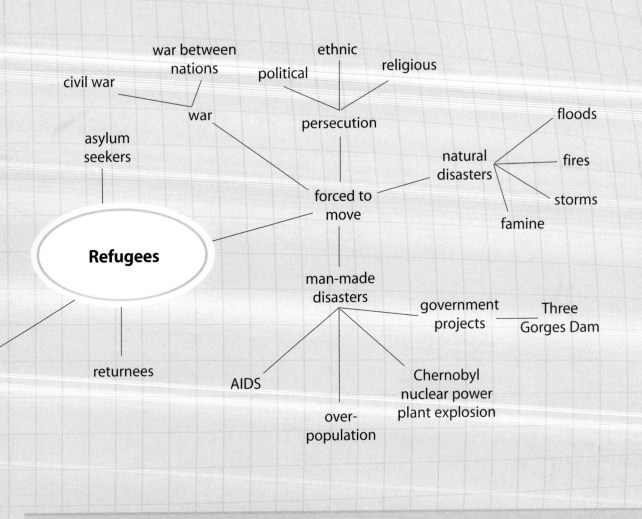

MAKE YOUR OWN CONCEPT WEB

A concept web is a useful summary tool. It can also be used to plan your research or help you write an essay or report. To make your own concept map, follow the steps below:

- You will need a large piece of unlined paper and a pencil.
- First, read through your source material, such as *Migrants and Refugees* in the Understanding Global Issues series.
- Write the main idea, or concept, in large letters in the center of the page.
- On a sheet of lined paper, jot down all words, phrases, or lists that you know are connected with the concept. Try to do this from memory.
- Look at your list. Can you group your words and phrases in certain topics or themes? Connect the different topics with lines to the center or to other "branches."
- Critique your concept web. Ask questions about the material on your concept web: Does it all make sense? Are all the links shown? Could there be other ways of looking at it? Is anything missing?
- What more do you need to find out? Develop questions for those areas you are still unsure about or where information is missing. Use these questions as a basis for further research.

Quiz

Multiple Choice

1. How many Africans were forced to move during the age of slavery?
   a) 1 million
   b) 12 million
   c) 50 million
   d) 100 million

2. How many refugees were there worldwide in 1955?
   a) 5 million
   b) 3.2 million
   c) 22 million
   d) 2.2 million

3. There have been more than how many wars since World War II?
   a) 500
   b) 50
   c) 200
   d) 150

4. The Cold War began in:
   a) 1960
   b) 1918
   c) 1945
   d) 1990

5. Which of the following organizations was founded in 1945?
   a) United Nations (UN)
   b) United Nations High Commissioner for Refugees (UNHCR)
   c) United Nations Children's Fund (UNICEF)
   d) United Nations Relief and Works Agency (UNRWA)

6. Which of the following is a migrant?
   a) A person who moves because a volcano has destroyed his or her home.
   b) A person who moves because of fear of mistreatment.
   c) A person who wishes for a job in another country.
   d) A person who moves because of war.

Where Did It Happen?

1. The Red Cross/Red Crescent was formed here in 1963.
2. This country saw 40 consecutive years of war—first external, then internal.
3. Iran and Pakistan have given shelter to more than five million refugees, most of them from this war-torn country.
4. The Chernobyl disaster occurred in this country.
5. The Three Gorges project is in this country.

True or False

1. Most refugees come from North American countries.
2. Most refugee situations occur because of natural disasters.
3. It is difficult to legally cross many of the present political borders.
4. Trafficking in migrants is illegal.
5. Migrants are usually a drain on the resources of their new country.
6. A refugee moves by choice.

Answers on page 53

Internet Resources

The following Web sites provide more information on migrants and refugees:

International Organization for Migration (IOM)
http://www.iom.int

IOM is the leading international organization for migration. IOM works with its international partners to meet the growing operational challenges of migration management, advance understanding of migration issues, encourage social and economic development through migration, and uphold the human dignity and well-being of migrants. The IOM Web site is a clear, informative source for information about the issues and problems facing migrants.

United Nations High Commissioner for Refugees (UNHCR)
http://www.unhcr.ch/cgi-bin/texis/vtx/home

UNHCR was established in 1951 to help the refugees of World War II. The UNHCR Web site contains the latest information about the state of refugees around the world.

United Nations Children's Fund (UNICEF)
http://www.unicef.org

UNICEF was created in 1946 to help children who were affected by the famine and disease caused by World War II. The UNICEF Web site contains information about the state of children around the world and describes many of the programs being conducted by UNICEF.

Some Web sites stay current longer than others. To find other migrant and refugee Web sites, enter terms such as "migrant," "refugee," or "displaced people" into a search engine.

Further Reading

International Federation of Red Cross and Red Crescent Societies. *World Disasters Report 2002.* Geneva, Switzerland: International Federation of Red Cross and Red Crescent Societies, 2002.

Mochizuki, Ken. *Passage to Freedom: The Sugihara Story.* New York: Lee & Low Books, 1997.

UNHCR. *The State of the World's Refugees 2000.* New York: Oxford University Press, 2001.

UNICEF. *The State of the World's Children 2000.* New York: United Nations, 2000.

Walker, Paul R. *True Tales of the Wild West.* Washington, D.C.: National Geographic Society, 2002.

Answers

Multiple Choice
1. b) 2. d) 3. d) 4. c) 5. a) 6. c)

Where Did It Happen?
1. Geneva, Switzerland 2. Angola 3. Afghanistan 4. Ukraine 5. China

True or False
1. F 2. F 3. T 4. T 5. F 6. F

Glossary

annexed: to take possession of something, usually by force or without permission

capitalist system: an economic system in which the production and distribution of wealth is controlled mainly by individuals and corporations

civil wars: a war between two groups within one country

communist system: a system within which all possessions are owned equally by all citizens

conscription: compulsory enrollment of people, especially for military service

defect: to leave one country or situation, often to go over to a rival

democracy: a government that is elected by the people and has an opposition

developing countries: those countries that are undergoing the process of industrialization

ethnic cleansing: the expulsion, imprisonment, or killing of ethnic minorities by a dominant majority group

genocide: the destruction of a racial, political, or cultural group

global warming: the warming of Earth due to greenhouse gases

gross national product: a measure of how much a country produces each year; indicates the economic health of a country

humanitarian: any effort or person that helps humanity as a whole

illegal immigrant: a person who migrates into a new country without permission

immigration: the movement of people into a new country

indentured: a contract binding one party into the service of another for a specified term

migration: moving from one place to another

multicultural: having a number of distinct cultures together

multi-ethnic: having people from a number of various ethnic backgrounds

nations: another term for countries

nongovernmental organizations: non-profit agencies that are independent from government

remittance: money sent to someone at a distance, usually family

repatriate: to return someone to his or her country of origin

urbanization: the movement of people from rural areas to cities

Index

Index

Photo Credits

Cover: Rwandan refugees return home (**R. Chalasani/Exile Images**); **Corel Corporation**: pages 2/3, 8, 22, 40, 47; **Digital Stock**: pages 30, 32; **DigitalVision**: page 33; **Exile Images**: pages 4, 10, 12, 14, 18, 25, 34, 35, 36, 38, 43 (**H. Davies**); **Getty/Taxi**: page 9; **International Labour Organization**: page 16 (**P. Deloche**); **International Red Cross**: pages 1, 20, 42; **MaXx Images**: page 21; **UN Photo 183790**: page 44 (**E. Kanalstein**); **UN Photo 200537**: page 45; **UNICEF Photo HQ00-0266**: page 39 (**Giacomo Pirozzi**); **Woolaroc Museum, Bartlesville, Oklahoma**: page 6.